Table of Contents

D0844059

perf top

My favorite place to start with perf is
perf top.

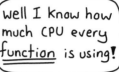

I like to run `perf top` on
machines when a program is
using 100% of the CPU and I
don't know why.

As an example, let's profile a really simple
program I wrote. It has a single function,
`run_awesome_function`, which is an infinite loop.

Here's the code
I ran. I called ⟹
the binary
`use_cpu`.

```
void run_awesome_function () {
    int x = 0;
    while (1) {
        x = x + 1;
    }
}
int main() { run_awesome_function(); }
```

While that's running, start `perf top`. It needs to run
as root, like every perf subcommand.

$ sudo perf top

4

perf top output

Here's what it looks like when I run perf top when use_cpu is running on my laptop:

```
①           ②                      ③
99.78%  use_cpu   [.] run_awesome_function
 0.02%  [kernel]  [k] update_vsyscall
 0.02%  [kernel]  [k] __softirqentry_text_start
```

① % of the CPU the function is using
② name of program or library
③ function name/symbol

This is telling us that 100% of the CPU time is being spent in run_awesome_function:

perf top can tell you about both:

★ functions in userspace programs
★ functions in the kernel

Here's what it looks in an example where the kernel is using a lot of CPU:

⌐ kernel functions!

```
27.70% [kernel]      [k] cpuidle_reflect
11.87% libxul.so     [.] _init
10.24% [kernel]      [k] _aesni_enc1
 6.75% [kernel]      [k] end_bio_extent_writepage
 3.94% [kernel]      [k] find_get_pages_contig
```

this function is doing encryption ("aes") because I'm writing to an encrypted filesystem

5

perf record

perf top is great for getting a quick idea of what's happening, but I often want to investigate more in depth.

perf record collects the same information as perf top, but it lets you save the data to analyze later. It saves it in a file called perf.data in your current directory.

There are 3 main ways to choose what process(es) to profile with perf record:

① perf record COMMAND ← start COMMAND and profile it until it exits

② perf record PID ← profile PID until you press ctrl+c

③ perf record -a ← profile every process until you press ctrl+c

There's a 4th hybrid thing you can do: If you specify both a PID (or -a) and a command, it'll profile the PID until the command exits. Like this:

PID COMMAND

perf record -p 8325 sleep 5

This useful trick lets you profile PID 8325 for 5 seconds!

collect tracing data with perf record

So far we've collected profiling data with perf like "what function is running?". When perf collects profiling data, it <u>samples</u> — it checks what function is running 100 times/second or something.

But perf can also record lots of different kinds of <u>events</u>. And when it records events, it <u>doesn't</u> sample — if you ask it to record system calls, it'll attempt to record every single system call.

Here are a few kinds of events:

→ system calls
→ sending network packets
→ reading from a block device (disk)
→ context switches/page faults
→ and you can make <u>any</u> kernel function into an event (that's called "kprobes")

" list every event with perf list "

For example, let's say you have a program making outbound network connections, but you don't know which program. perf can help!

This perf incantation records every time a program connects to a web server (the connect system call), and it also records the <u>stack trace</u> that led up to the syscall.

g means collect stack trace

```
perf record -e syscalls:sys_enter_connect -ag
```

Being able to take a syscall/page fault/disk write and trace it back to the exact code that caused it is pretty magical.

7

analyzing perf record data

There are 3 ways to analyze a `perf.data` file
generated by perf record:

perf report displays a quick
interactive report showing you which
functions are used the most

self	command	shared object	symbol
0.01%	use_cpu	[kernel.kallsyms]	[k] update_wall_time
99.74%	use_cpu	use_cpu	[.] run_awesome_function

~100% of the time is spent in this function!

perf annotate will tell you which
assembly instructions your program
is spending most of its time
executing (be careful, can be off
by one instruction)

assembly instructions!

```
|        Disassembly of section .text:
|
|        00000000004004d6 <run_awesome_function>:
|        run_awesome_function():
|          push    %rbp
|          mov     %rsp,%rbp
|          movl    $0x0,-0x4(%rbp)
99.68 |  b:  addl   $0x1,-0x4(%rbp)
 0.32 |     ↑ jmp   b
```

this add instruction
is where all the
time's being spent

perf script prints out all the
samples perf collected as text so
you can run scripts on the output
to do analysis. Like the flamegraph
script on the next page! ⇨

```
use_cpu 13650 12337 096592:    657702 cycles:ppp:
                  4e1 run_awesome_function (use_cpu)
                  4f5 main (use_cpu)
               20830 __libc_start_main (libc-2.23.so)
    8fe258d4c544155 [unknown] ([unknown])
```

instruction

stack trace

symbol

8

flamegraphs

Flamegraphs are an awesome way to visualize profiling data, profiling data. They were invented and popularized by Brendan Gregg.

Here's what they look like:

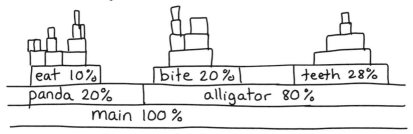

They're constructed from lots (usually thousands) of stack traces sampled from a program. This one above means that 20% of the stack traces started with $\begin{bmatrix} main \\ panda \end{bmatrix}$ and 28% started with $\begin{bmatrix} main \\ alligator \\ teeth \end{bmatrix}$.

To generate flamegraphs, get

⋛ github.com/brendangregg/Flamegraph ⋛

and put it in your PATH. Once you have that, here's how to generate a flamegraph:

```
$ sudo perf script | stackcollapse-perf.pl
                   | flamegraph.pl > graph.svg
```

open this in your browser!

(this is the same perf script from the previous page)

perf + node.js or Java =

Normally with interpreted languages like node.js, perf will tell you which interpreter function is running but not which Javascript function is running. But:

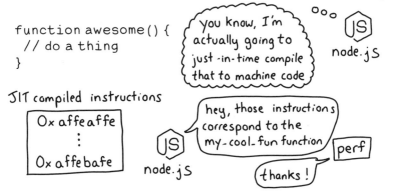

JS ☕ Java — We can help tell perf what's going on!

"just in time"

This works because both node and Java have a JIT compiler.

```
function awesome() {
  // do a thing
}
```

you know, I'm actually going to just-in-time compile that to machine code

JS node.js

JIT compiled instructions

```
Ox affe affe
  :
Ox affe bafe
```

JS node.js

hey, those instructions correspond to the my-cool-fun function

perf

thanks!

node.js communicates with perf by writing a file called
   /tmp/perf-$PID.map
How to set that up:

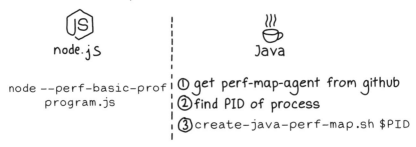

JS
node.js

☕
Java

```
node --perf-basic-prof
   program.js
```

① get perf-map-agent from github
② find PID of process
③ create-java-perf-map.sh $PID

10

Why are there kernel functions in my stack trace?

Sometimes you'll get a stack trace from perf, and it'll mix functions from your program (like __getdents64) and functions from the kernel (like btrfs_real_readdir).
This is normal!

Example:

```
find 27968 97997.204322:    707897 cycles:pp:
      7fffc034eac7 read_extent_buffer ([kernel.kallsyms])
      7fffc032e4f7 btrfs_real_readdir ([kernel.kallsyms])
      7fff81229eb8 iterate_dir ([kernel.kallsyms])
      7fff8122a359 sys_getdents ([kernel.kallsyms])
      7fff81850fc8 entry_SYSCALL_64_fastpath ([kernel.kallsyms])
         c88eb __getdents64 (/lib/x86_64-linux-gnu/libc-2.23.so)
```
↑ function from your program

It usually means either your program did a system call or there was a page fault, and it's telling you exactly which kernel functions were called as a result of that syscall.

For example, because I'm using the btrfs filesystem, in this case the getdents syscall calls the btrfsf_real_readdir function. Neat!

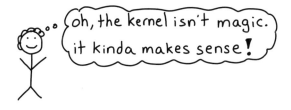
oh, the kernel isn't magic. it kinda makes sense!

★ perf cheat sheet ★

important command line arguments:

♥ what data to get♥
- -F: pick sample frequency
- -g: record stack traces
- -e: choose events to record

♥ what program(s) to look at♥
- -a: entire system
- -p: specify a PID
- COMMAND: run this cmd

★ perf top: get updates live! ★

```
# Sample CPUs at 49 Hertz, show top symbols:
perf top -F 49

# Sample CPUs, show top process names and segments:
perf top -ns comm,dso
```
⎫
⎬ sampling
⎭

```
# Count system calls by process, refreshing every 1 second:
perf top -e raw_syscalls:sys_enter -ns comm -d 1

# Count sent network packets by process, rolling output:
stdbuf -oL perf top -e net:net_dev_xmit -ns comm | strings
```
⎫
⎬ event tracing
⎭

★ perf stat : count events! CPU counters! ★

```
# CPU counter statistics for COMMAND:
perf stat COMMAND

# *Detailed* CPU counter statistics for COMMAND:
perf stat -ddd command

# Count system calls for PID, until Ctrl-C:
perf stat -e 'syscalls:sys_enter_*' -p PID

# Count block device I/O events for the entire system, for 10
seconds:
perf stat -e 'block:*' -a sleep 10
```

★ Reporting ★

```
# Show perf.data in an ncurses browser:
perf report

# Show perf.data as a text report:
perf report --stdio

# List all events from perf.data:
perf script

# Annotate assembly instructions from perf.data
# with percentages
perf annotate [--stdio]
```

★ perf trace : trace system calls & other events ★

```
# Trace syscalls system wide          # Trace syscalls for PID
perf trace                            perf trace -p PID
```

★ perf record: record profiling data ★

← records into
perf.data file

```
# Sample CPU functions for COMMAND at 99 Hertz:
perf record -F 99 COMMAND
```

```
# Sample CPU functions for PID, until Ctrl-C:
perf record -p PID
```

```
# Sample CPU functions for PID, for 10 seconds:
perf record -p PID sleep 10
```

```
# Sample CPU stack traces for PID, for 10 seconds:
perf record -p PID -g -- sleep 10
```

```
# Sample CPU stack traces for PID, using DWARF to unwind stack:
perf record -p PID --call-graph dwarf
```

★ perf record : record tracing data ★

← records into
perf.data file

```
# Trace new processes, until Ctrl-C:
perf record -e sched:sched_process_exec -a
```

```
# Trace all context switches, until Ctrl-C:
perf record -e context-switches -a
```

```
# Trace all context switches with stack traces, for 10
seconds:
perf record -e context-switches -ag -- sleep 10
```

```
# Trace all page faults with stack traces, until Ctrl-C:
perf record -e page-faults -ag
```

★ adding new trace events ★

```
# Add a tracepoint for kernel function tcp_sendmsg():
perf probe 'tcp_sendmsg'
```

```
# Trace previously created probe:
perf record -e probe:tcp_sendmsg -a
```

```
# Add a tracepoint for myfunc() and include the retval as a string:
perf probe 'myfunc%return +0($retval):string'
```

need kernel debuginfo

```
# Trace previous probe when size > 0:
perf record -e probe:tcp_sendmsg --filter 'size > 0' -a
```

```
# Add a tracepoint for do_sys_open() with the filename as a string:
perf probe 'do_sys_open filename:string'
```

13

perf stat: CPU counters

If you're writing high-performance programs, there are a lot of CPU/hardware-level events you might be interested in counting:

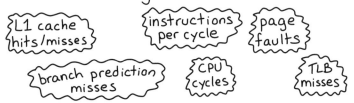

- L1 cache hits/misses
- instructions per cycle
- page faults
- branch prediction misses
- CPU cycles
- TLB misses

You might wonder:

how can I tell what the L1 cache hit rate is though?? I'd need to look INSIDE THE CPU?!

hardware counters! —

Basically, Linux can ask your CPU to start recording various statistics:

(perf) hey can you count L1 cache hits + misses?

on it!

Linux

hey can you count L1 cache hits + misses?

on it!

CPU

As an example, here's part of the output of `perf stat -ddd ls`

d is for detailed

```
$ sudo perf stat -ddd ls -R /
Performance counter stats for 'ls -R /':
         3849.615096      task-clock (msec)         #    0.535 CPUs utilized
              26,120      context-switches          #    0.007 M/sec
                 342      page-faults               #    0.089 K/sec
           8,583,744,395 cycles                     #    2.230 GHz
          10,337,612,795 instructions               #    1.20  insns per cycle
           1,987,339,660 branches                   #  516.244 M/sec
              20,738,878 branch-misses              #    1.04% of all branches
           2,883,947,626 dTLB-loads                 #  749.152 M/sec

         7.192555725 seconds time elapsed
```

10 billion instructions happen **fast**.

branch prediction stats

perf stat : count any event

You can actually count lots of different events with perf stat — the same events you can record with perf record!

Here are a couple of examples of using perf stat on ls -R (which lists files recursively, so it makes lots of system calls):

① count context switches between the kernel and userspace!

② count system calls!

wildcard

```
$ sudo perf stat -e 'syscalls:sys_enter_*' ls -R /
        > /dev/null
```

I ran these through sort -n to get a top list

count	system call
8,028	syscalls:sys_enter_newlstat
15,167	syscalls:sys_enter_write
254,755	syscalls:sys_enter_close
254,777	syscalls:sys_enter_open
509,496	syscalls:sys_enter_newfstat
509,598	syscalls:sys_enter_getdents

directory entries

perf stat does introduce some overhead. Counting *every* system call for find made the program run up to ⟨6 times⟩ slower in my brief experiments.

I think as long as you only count a few different events (like just the syscalls:sys_enter_open event) it should be fine. I don't 100% understand why there's so much overhead here though.

perf trace

strace is an awesome Linux debugging tool that traces system calls. It has one problem though:

perf trace traces system calls, but with <u>way less</u> overhead. It's safe to run in production, unlike strace.

There are 2 disadvantages though (as of Linux 4.4):

① sometimes it drops system calls (this is sort of an advantage since it limits overhead)

② it won't show you the strings that are being read/written.

Here's a comparison of both strace and perf trace output, on the same program:

{perf trace}   no string!   {strace}   string!

```
brk(brk: 0x2397000)
write(fd: 2, buf: 0x28
read(buf: 0x7ffd77b0a8d7, 1
ioctl(cmd: TCGETS, arg: ...
ioctl(cmd: TCSETSW, arg: ...
```

```
brk(brk: 0x2397000)                      = 0x23
write(2, "bork@kiwi:~", 13) = 13
read(0, "\4", 1)                = 1
ioctl(0, TCGETS, arg: 0x7ffd77b0a
ioctl(0, SNDCTL_TMR_STOP or TCSETSW
```

These have the same write system call, but only strace actually shows you what string was written.

Recently I used perf trace, and it told me Docker was calling stat on (200,000) files, which was a VERY USEFUL CLUE that helped me figure out that Docker gets container sizes by looking at every file. I used perf trace because I didn't want to deal with strace's overhead!

16

how perf works: overview

Now that we know how to use perf, let's see how it works!

The perf system is split into 2 parts:

① a program in userspace called `perf`
② a system in the Linux kernel

When you run `perf record`, `perf stat`, or `perf top` to get information about a program, here's what happens:

→ perf asks the kernel to collect information.

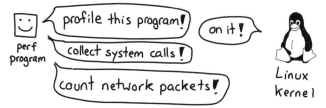

→ the kernel gets samples/traces/CPU counters from the programs perf asks about.

→ perf displays the data back to you in a (hopefully) useful way.

So here's the big picture:

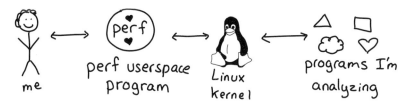

on kernel versions

perf works really closely with the Linux kernel. This means a couple of things:

→ You need to install a version of perf that exactly matches your kernel version.
On Ubuntu, you can do that with:

```
sudo apt-get install linux-tools-$(uname -r)
```

→ perf's features (and sometimes command-line options) change between kernel versions.

The first version of perf was in Linux 2.6.

This also means that there's a perf documentation folder in the Linux git repository! You can see it on github:

github.com/torvalds/linux/tree/master/tools/perf/Documentation

Some of the cool things in there:

perf.data file format spec
how to use perf's built-in Python interpreter (?) to write scripts
all the man pages for each perf subcommand

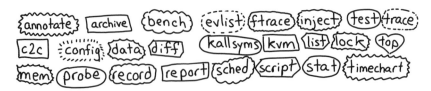

how profiling with perf works

The Linux kernel has a built-in sampling profiler.

Linux: I checked what function the program was running 50,000 times and here are the results!

How does Linux know which functions your program is running though? Well, the Linux kernel is in charge of scheduling.

That means that at all times it has a list of every process and the address of the CPU instruction that each process is currently running. That address is called the instruction pointer.

Here's what the information the Linux kernel has looks like:

command	PID	thread ID	instruction pointer
python	2379	2379	0x00759d2d
bash	1229	1229	0x00123456
use_cpu	4991	4991	0xabababab
use_cpu	4991	4992	0xababdddd

Sometimes perf can't figure out how to turn an instruction pointer address into a function name. Here's an example of what that looks like:

?? mysterious address !!

self	command	shared object	symbol	
0.00%	nodejs	nodejs	[.]	0x00000759d20
0.00%	V8 WorkerThread	[kernel.kallsyms]	[k]	hrtimer_active

which programming languages can perf profile?

The way perf usually figures out what function your programs are running is:

① get the program's <u>instruction pointer address</u>
② get a copy of the program's stack
③ unwind the stack to find the address of the current function call
④ use the program's <u>symbol table</u> to figure out the name of the symbol that address corresponds to!

The important thing to understand is that perf will by default give you a symbol from the program symbol table. That means perf won't give you function names for binaries where the symbols are stripped.

Here's how perf can help you, broken down by programming language:

C, C++, Go, Rust
perf will tell you what function is running

node.js Java/Scala/clojure **JVM languages**
perf can use an alternate method to find the "real" function (like we explained on page 10)

Python, Ruby, PHP, other interpreted languages
perf will tell you about the interpreter (can still be useful!)

perf: under the hood

It's often useful to have a basic understanding of how our tools are implemented. So let's look at the interface the userspace tool (perf) uses to talk to the Linux kernel. Here's what happens, basically:

① perf calls the perf_event_open system call
② the kernel writes events to a ring buffer in userspace
③ perf reads events off that ring buffer and displays them to you somehow

What's a ring buffer?

Basically, it's important to use a limited amount of memory for profiling events. So the kernel allocates a fixed amount of money:

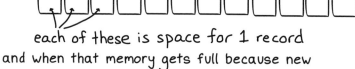

each of these is space for 1 record

and when that memory gets full because new records are being written faster than perf can read them...

whoops! we're out of space. guess I can't write more events!

Linux

So if you see warnings from perf about events being dropped, that's what happening.

the perf_event_open system call

This system call is how perf asks the Linux kernel to start sampling or tracing.

Here's the system call's signature, from man perf_event_open:

```
int perf_event_open(struct perf_event_attr *attr,
                    pid_t pid, int cpu, int group_fd,
                    unsigned long flags);
```

PID & CPU to look at. Can be "all of them".

this is where most of the arguments are.

I don't find this man page all that useful for day-to-day perf usage. But! Did you know that the perf CLI tool isn't the only program that uses the perf_event_open syscall?

The bcc project is a toolkit for writing advanced profiling tools using eBPF: ⬤ github.com/iovisor/bcc

With bcc, you can relatively easily use perf_event_open to create your own custom profiling/tracing events! And then you can write code to aggregate/display them any way you want.

Search for BCC_PERF_OUTPUT in the bcc docs to learn more.